TERRIFIC TONGUES!

Maria Gianferrari

Illustrated by Jia Liu

BOYDS MILLS PRESS
An Imprint of Highlights
Honesdale, Pennsylvania

It's a straw.

It's a nose.

It's a mop.

It's a sword.

It's a . . . ToNGUE.

STICK OUT
YOUR TONGUE!

If you had a tongue like a sword, you might be a . . .

WOODPECKER!

The red-bellied woodpecker's tongue is three times as long as its beak, and as sharp as a sword. It uses its barbed tongue to stab beetle larvae and other insects that burrow beneath tree bark.

If you had a tongue like a straw,
you might be a . . .

MOTH!

Moths sip flower nectar with their long, tubelike tongues. When they're not eating, moths roll up their tongues like garden hoses. The Darwin's hawkmoth has a body only four inches long, yet its tongue is twelve inches—that's three times as long as its body.

If you had a tongue like a party blower, you might be a . . .

FROG!

The North American bullfrog's tongue unrolls like a party blower. It's sticky, for catching insects, crayfish, snakes, turtles, frogs, and even ducklings.

If you had a tongue like a nose, you might be a . . .

SNAKE!

A snake's tongue helps it smell. It sticks out its forked tongue to collect chemicals in the environment. The chemicals are then absorbed by two pits on the roof of its mouth called the Jacobson's organ. The Jacobson's organ sends a message to the snake's brain, letting it know whether it's smelling food, danger, or a mate.

If you had a tongue like a mop,
you might be a . . .

BAT!

When the Pallas's long-tongued bat sticks its tongue out for drinking, hairs on its surface pop out to absorb the nectar, like the fibers on a string mop.

If you had a
tongue like a washcloth,
you might be an . . .

OKAPI!

An okapi's tongue is like a washcloth. Okapi tongues are so long that okapis can use them to wash their eyes and ears.

If you had a
tongue like a whip,
you might be an . . .

The giant anteater's tongue is as long and fast as a whip. It flicks its tongue in and out of insect nests up to 160 times a minute. Count to one. SNAP! SNAP! SNAP! The anteater's tongue has already snapped in and out of the nest almost three times.

If you had a tongue
like a windshield wiper,
you might be a . . .

GECKO!

Mourning geckos
don't have eyelids.
Their tongues swish
over their eyes, like
windshield wipers,
to keep them clean.

If you had a tongue
like an arrow,
you might be a . . .

CHAMELEON!

The chameleon's tongue hurls toward its prey, as quick as a toy arrow shot from a bow. The tip of the chameleon's tongue forms a suction cup, slurping up prey as large as lizards and small birds.

If you had a tongue like an air conditioner, you might be a . . .

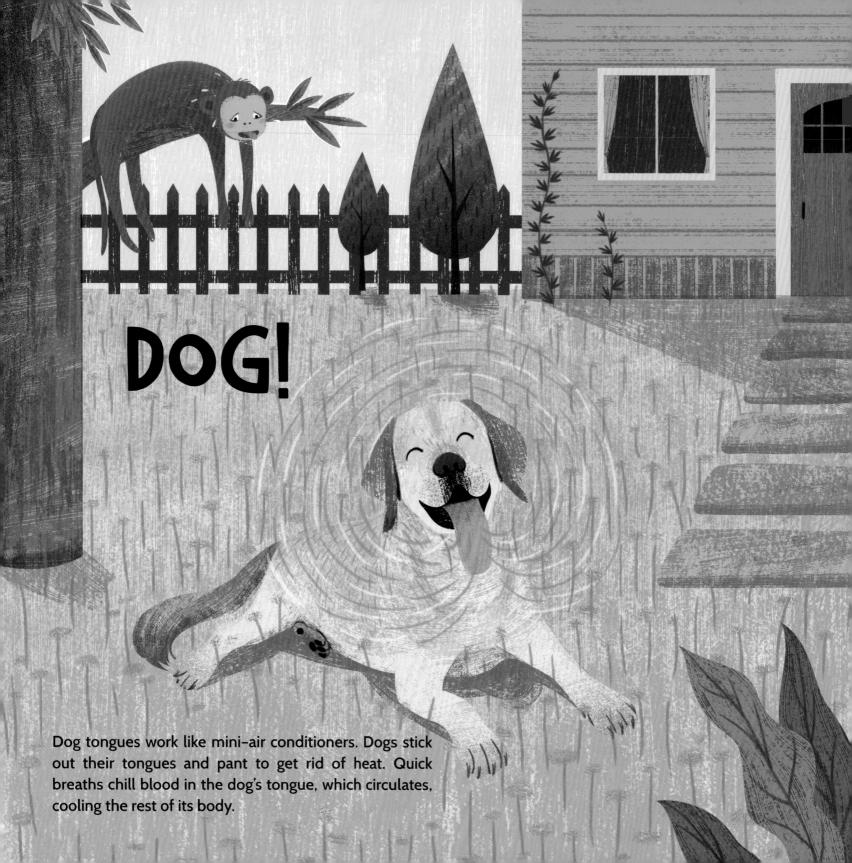

DOG!

Dog tongues work like mini-air conditioners. Dogs stick out their tongues and pant to get rid of heat. Quick breaths chill blood in the dog's tongue, which circulates, cooling the rest of its body.

If you had TWO tongues,
you might be an . . .

OCTOPUS!

The common octopus uses its tongues like a carpenter uses tools. An octopus chips at the shell of its prey with its sharp beak, then it scrapes its tongue back and forth inside the shell like a rasp. If filing doesn't work, it then uses another tongue-like organ to drill through the shell.

If you had a tongue that could lick, taste, blow bubbles with gum, talk, and whistle, you'd be . . .

YOU!

Your tongue can lick:
Your tongue has many muscles, so it can move up, down, side to side, and out—perfect for licking lollipops and ice-cream cones!

Your tongue can taste:
You have bumps on your tongue that contain thousands of tiny sensors called taste buds. What if your chocolate ice cream tasted like . . . popcorn? Without taste buds, everything might taste the same; with taste buds, your tongue can taste sweet chocolate, salty pretzels, sour lemons, and bitter medicine.

Your tongue can talk:
All the muscles in your tongue help you talk. Say "scissors."
Now hold your tongue down with two fingers and repeat it. See?

Let's talk tongue twisters!

Say this as fast as you can:

A Tudor who tooted a flute
tried to tutor two tooters to toot.
Said the two to their tutor,
"Is it harder to toot
or to tutor two tooters to toot?"

YOUR TONGUE iS TERRiFiC TOo!

Tongues
**STAB,
SUCK,
GRAB.**

Tongues
**CLEAN,
MOP,
PREEN.**

Tongues
**SNATCH,
SMELL,
CATCH,
TELL.**

Tongues **COOL**.
Tongues **RULE!**
TONGUES ARE TERRIFIC!

MORE ABOUT THESE TERRIFIC TONGUES!

A red-bellied woodpecker's tongue is so long that when it retracts, it goes down the woodpecker's throat, over its skull, and into its nostril! They live in the eastern United States.

Because of its twelve-inch tongue, the Darwin's hawkmoth of Madagascar, named after Charles Darwin, is the only insect able to pollinate the star-shaped comet orchid. A moth's tongue is called a proboscis (*pro-BAA-sis* or *pro-BOS-kiss*), as are the tongues of bees and butterflies.

Unlike a human's tongue, a frog's tongue is attached at the front of the mouth and works like a catapult. It's soft and mushy until the frog spies its prey, then its muscles become rigid—zipping forward and zapping back in less than 15/100ths of a second. That's quicker than you can sneeze!

A snake's forked tongue helps it smell in two ways. Snakes follow a scent trail by touching the ground with their tongues, but when they smell the air, they flick their tongues from side to side, enabling them to sample more air. A snake's forked tongue allows it to collect chemicals from two different places at the same time.

A resident of Central and South America, a Pallas's long-tongued bat is only two inches long, with a tongue twice as long as its head. The hairs on the bat's tongue lie flat until it extends its tongue for drinking. When the tongue is fully extended, blood rushes into the hairs, raising them up.

An okapi's long tongue is prehensile, which means it's used for grabbing things. It's also sticky, so it's perfect for plucking faraway leaves from their branches. Okapis live in the rainforests of the Democratic Republic of the Congo in Central Africa.

Giant anteaters live in Central and South America. Their tongues are covered with sticky saliva to help them trap insects—more than 30,000 ants and termites a day! Their tongues are nearly two feet long—that's as long as two rulers in a row!

Gecko tongues aren't just for cleaning. Like snakes, geckos also have a Jacobson's organ, and flick out their tongues to smell and taste their environment. But gecko tongues are notched, not forked. Mourning geckos live in coastal areas along the Indian and Pacific Oceans.

A chameleon's tongue is spring-loaded. Blink your eyes. Before you've blinked once, the chameleon has already caught its prey! Using high-speed video, scientists have observed that an average chameleon's tongue can travel twenty feet per second, or approximately thirteen miles per hour. Insects beware!

Dog tongues help regulate body temperature, but they're also used for eating, drinking, healing wounds, and grooming. But best of all, dogs' tongues are for kisses!

An octopus tongue, called a radula, is covered with tiny sawlike teeth for filing prey from their shells. The drill, called the salivary papilla, contains chemicals that also help to erode, or wear down, shells. The common octopus lives in tropical and temperate waters worldwide.

EVEN MORE FUN TONGUES!

Tigers, lions, and other wildcats have tongues with barbs as sharp as knives for scraping meat from bones or feathers from flesh.

Yellow-bellied sapsuckers, a type of woodpecker, have feathery, paintbrush-like tongues for lapping sap.

Barbs on a cat's tongue make it multi-purpose: it's a washcloth, towel, and comb all rolled into one. When a cat licks, small spikes on its tongue help wash its fur, dry it like a towel, and smooth it like a comb.

Ruby-throated hummingbirds drink nectar with their grooved and forked tongues. The outer grooves draw up the nectar like straws.

Madagascan moths drink the tears of sleeping birds with their barbed, harpoon-shaped tongues. Scientists think they're searching for salt.

Northern flickers, members of the woodpecker family, can catch thousands of ants with their gooey tongues.

Like snakes, komodo dragons have long, forked tongues as well as Jacobson's organs to smell and detect prey from miles away.

Cows lack upper front teeth, so their rough tongues curl around grass and hay to rip food apart.

Für Anya und ihre Zungen —MG

Many thanks to my family—my mom, dad, and brother—who have supported me throughout the years as I grew into the person I wanted to be. —JL

Boyds Mills Press
An Imprint of Highlights
815 Church Street
Honesdale, Pennsylvania 18431

Printed in China
ISBN: 978-1-62091-784-8
Library of Congress Control Number: 2017942210

First edition
The text of this book is set in Cuca.
The illustrations are digital.

10 9 8 7 6 5 4 3 2 1